Teyrnas y Glo
Coal's Domain

Golwg Hanesyddol ar Fywyd ym Meysydd Glo Cymru | *Historical Glimpses of Life in the Welsh Coalfields*

gan | *by*

Bill Jones
Amgueddfa Diwydiant a Môr Cymru
Welsh Industrial and Maritime Museum

Beth Thomas
Amgueddfa Werin Cymru
Welsh Folk Museum

AMGUEDDFA GENEDLAETHOL CYMRU
NATIONAL MUSEUM OF WALES
CAERDYDD/CARDIFF 1993

First published in March, 1993 © National Museum of Wales Cathays Park Cardiff CF1 3NP ISBN 0 7200 0380 6 Production: Hywel G. Rees Design: ARB, Cardiff Typesetting: Cardiff Typesetting Co Type: Baskerville 9/10 point Printing: South Western Printers, Caerphilly	Cyhoeddwyd gyntaf ym mis Mawrth, 1993 (h) Amgueddfa Genedlaethol Cymru Parc Cathays Caerdydd CF1 3NP ISBN 0 7200 0380 6 Cynhyrchu: Hywel G. Rees Graffeg: ARB, Caerdydd Cysodi: Cardiff Typesetting Co Teip: Baskerville 9/10 pwynt Argraffu: South Western Printers, Caerffili

Rhagarweiniad

Am dros ganrif a hanner bellach, bu twf a dirywiad y diwydiant glo, ynghyd â'u canlyniadau cymdeithasol ac economaidd, yn llywodraethu hanes Cymru. Oherwydd y galw anniwall am lo, tyfodd cymunedau newydd a bywiog eu diwylliant ym meysydd glo De a Gogledd Cymru, mewn rhannau o'r wlad lle nad oedd dim ond ffermdai gwasgaredig cyn hynny. Heddiw, gyda dirywiad y diwydiant anferthol hwn (a gyflogai bron i 250,000 o bobl yn ei anterth yn 1913), fe wêl y cymunedau hyn newidiadau gyda'r mwyaf syfrdanol a sylfaenol yn eu hanes.

Ers dros chwarter canrif bu Amgueddfa Genedlaethol Cymru, yn yr Amgueddfa Werin a'r Amgueddfa Diwydiant a Môr, yn casglu tystiolaeth lafar a gweledol i ddogfennu hanes y diwydiant glo a chymunedau glofaol yng Nghymru. Tyfodd yr archifau hyn bellach yn ffynhonnell gyfoethog o ddeunydd sydd ar gael i unrhyw ymchwilydd a chanddo ddiddordeb yn y pwnc. Pwrpas y llyfryn hwn yw cyflwyno'r casgliadau hyn i'r darllenydd cyffredin, trwy roi cipolwg ar ffordd o fyw sydd bellach yn diflannu.

Wrth lunio'r llyfryn, nid oedd yn fwriad gennym ysgrifennu hanes manwl a ffeithiol. Yn hytrach, tynnwyd o'n harchifau ddetholiad o dystiolaeth lafar a lluniau i fwrw goleuni ar yr agweddau pwysicaf ar fywyd yn y meysydd glo ddechrau'r ganrif. Craidd y llyfryn yw profiadau'r bobl a fu'n byw yn yr ardaloedd hyn, wedi eu disgrifio yn eu geiriau eu hunain a'u hategu â thystiolaeth ffotograffig. Hyd y gwyddom, ychydig o'r deunydd hwn a gyhoeddwyd o'r blaen. Nid ydym wedi rhoi sylwadaeth; gadewir i'r 'lleisiau' siarad drostynt eu hunain. O ganlyniad, fe welir bod y dystiolaeth lafar yn adlewyrchu gwahaniaethau ieithyddol a diwylliannol oddi mewn i'r ardaloedd glofaol. Lle bo'r dystiolaeth wreiddiol yn Gymraeg, darperir cyfieithad; gadawyd yr enghreifftiau Saesneg heb eu cyfieithu, gan y byddai eu trosglwyddo i Gymraeg safonol yn dileu'r naws llafar sydd yn rhan mor hanfodol o'r dystiolaeth.

Gobeithir y bydd cynnwys y llyfryn hwn o ddiddordeb i'r darllenydd cyffredin a hefyd o werth addysgiadol. Hoffem ddiolch i bawb a gyfrannodd at ein harchifau, trwy rannu eu profiadau a rhoi neu fenthyg lluniau. Mewn sawl ystyr, mae'r dalennau canlynol yn deyrnged iddynt hwy a'u ffordd o fyw.

Introduction

The history of Wales during the past one hundred and fifty years has been dominated by the growth and subsequent decline of the coal industry, and their social and economic consequences. Because of the almost insatiable demand for Welsh coal, new and vibrant communities, with their own distinctive life-style and culture, grew up in hitherto unpopulated areas of the two coalfields of North and South Wales. Today, with the decline of this once gargantuan industry (which at its peak in 1913 employed nearly 250,000 men and women), these communities are experiencing changes as fundamental and dramatic as any during the course of their unique yet relatively short history.

Over the decades the National Museum of Wales, at the Welsh Folk Museum and the Welsh Industrial and Maritime Museum, has been collecting oral and visual evidence to document the history of coalmining and coalfield communities in Wales. These archives have grown into a rich resource which is available for consultation by anyone interested in the subject. The purpose of this booklet is to introduce the collections to the general reader by presenting a series of 'glimpses' of a way of life that is now disappearing.

In compiling this booklet we have not set out to write a full and factual history. Rather, from our archive we have selected first hand accounts and images to illustrate some of the central features of life in the Welsh coalfields during the first half of the twentieth century. The focus is primarily on the experiences of people who have lived in these areas, as described in their own words and recorded in photographs, many of which, to the best of our knowledge, have not been published before. We have refrained from providing a commentary; the individual 'voices' have been left to speak for themselves. As such the oral evidence reflects cultural and linguistic differences. Where the original testimony was recorded in Welsh, we have provided a translation; the English-language extracts have been left in their original language and idiom.

It is hoped that the contents of this booklet will be of interest to the general reader and of value as an educational resource. We would like to thank all those people who have contributed to our archives, by sharing their experiences and donating or loaning photographs. In many ways the following pages are a tribute to them and the lives they have lived.

Y Cymunedau *The Communities*

Y meysydd glo yn eu hanterth. Glofa'r Glamorgan, Llwynypia, tua 1920.
Coal mining and the landscape it created. Glamorgan Colliery, Llwynypia, about 1920.

They were coming to the Rhondda from all over, weren't they? From Bristol and Somerset to work in the mines. It was the local Klondike sort of thing wasn't it? But not much of a Klondike about it now. Well, you had the Cambrian up here - well there was three thousand men working there, isn't it? There's none there now. The Llwynypia colliery which was known as the Scotch colliery - about three thousand working there. That's shut. The Naval colliery in Pen-y-graig - about two thousand - that's shut. You know, only in this locality I've been talking about, you're talking about fifteen to twenty thousand men. Only in a small locality like this! And of course, all the way up the valley the same.

Gŵr o Donypandy, ganed 1906
Tonypandy man, born 1906

Y Cymunedau *The Communities*

Golygfa o Droed-y-rhiw, Merthyr, tua 1900.
A Troed-y-rhiw, Merthyr, scene about 1900.

Odd 'i'n amsar glawd yn y wlad pyr'ny chwel. Cyflog yn fach a'r pwlla 'ma yn 'u bri. A'i ddæth e lan 'ma . Lan 'ma ddæth e fel ostlar. Dishgwl ar ôl y ceffyla odd a i ddychra. A i æth lawr dan ddaear weti'ny. A yma yn ni wedi sefyll byth.

They were poor times in the countryside then, you see. The pay was poor, and these pits were at their height. So he came up here. He came up here as an ostler. Looking after the horses he was to start with. And then after that he went down underground. And we've been here ever since.

Gŵr o Ferndale, ganed 1882
Ferndale man, born 1882

My father came from Somerset, and my mother came from Devon. Well of course, the mines were developing, and the railways were developing, and of course there was no money working on the farms in the country, so that's what happened. And thousands like them...

Gŵr o Gwm Ogwr, ganed 1906
Ogmore Vale man, born 1906

'Sdim dowt bod y ffordd ma tai yn cál 'u adeiladu 'eddi yn neud gwaniath. Achos gwetwch chi pan bo *row* o dai 'da chi, ma fa bron yn orfodiath i chi fyw'n agosach at ych cymdogion, yndywa? Werth ych chi mwy ar ben ych gilydd na bo chi'n cál tai nawr mwn *terrace* a 'mach o *railings* ringddoch chi. Wel symo 'wnna ar gâl mewn *row!* Unwath chi ar y stepyn drws, chi bron ar stepyn drws y fenyw drws nesa!

No doubt that the way houses are built today makes a difference. Because when you live in a row, you're almost forced to live closer to your neighbours, aren't you? You're more on top of one another than if you had a house in a terrace with railings between you. Well that's not to be had in a row! Once you're on the doorstep, you're almost on the doorstep of the woman next door!

Gwraig o Bont-rhyd-y-fen, ganed 1925
Pont-rhyd-y-fen woman, born 1925

Y Cymunedau *The Communities*

Dozens of butchers' shops and grocers' shops, drapers' shops, shoe shops - they were all there. But today, very few. Very few. In those days we had Liptons' then, we had a dairy, Maypole, Home and Colonial, Thomas and Evans, the Co-op, the Newmarket Stores. All in Tonypandy. Clydach Vale was a busy little centre in those days. Blaen Clydach, quite a number of shops there in those days. Well as many shops in Blaen Clydach at that time as what is in Tonypandy today, I think. It was a little gold mine in the old days. Of course, the collieries was working then. Cambrian was working, Blaen Clydach was working full swing. Those were the days...

Gŵr o Ben-y-graig, ganed 1908
Pen-y-graig man, born 1908

Stryd Dunraven, Tonypandy, tua 1914
Dunraven Street, Tonypandy, about 1914

Cwm Clydach yn y 1930au
Clydach Vale in the 1930s

Gweithio ar y Glo *Working the Coal*

Bachgen o lôwr o'r enw 'Hapenny' o ardal Tonypandy, tua 1920
Collier boy named 'Hapenny', from the Tonypandy area, about 1920

Hen ac ifanc yng ngwaith Ferndale. Un o gyfres o luniau a dynnwyd yn ystod yr ymweliad Brenhinol â De Cymru yn 1907.
Young and old at Ferndale Colliery. One of a series of photographs taken during the Royal visit to South Wales in 1907

Mother had bought me, what they call underground a box and jack. A tommy box and a can to carry your tea. And she'd have bought that the day before I was fourteen. So I started to work at fourteen in 1907.
Glöwr o Hook, Penfro, ganed 1893
Miner from Hook, Pembrokeshire, born 1893

I had plenty of opportunities to stay on in school, but all I wanted to do was to go to the pits, because my butties were there...
Glöwr o Garndiffaith, ganed 1895
Gadawodd yr ysgol yn 13 oed
Garndiffaith miner, born 1895. Left school at 13

We were anxious to go, I can tell you! I was so excited about it, I didn't sleep the night before. I wanted to know what time it was, wanting to get up. But I've changed my tune since then though! Oh aye!
Glöwr o Rymni, ganed 1881
Rhymni miner, born 1881

Gweithio ar y Glo *Working the Coal*

Gweithwyr ifainc o Bwll Pochin, tua 1910
Young colliers from Pochin Colliery, about 1910

Wel odd dim byd arall i gâl 'ma chi'n gwel'. Dim byd. Beth arall odd 'da chi? Dim ond gwaith glo. Meddylwch am grotyn yn cwnnu am wech ar gloch y bore, a mynd lawr i ben y gwaith yndife. Ag yn y gwaith allech chi weud o 'anner awr 'di wech sbo'i 'annar awr 'di pump yn y nos a wech ar gloch y nos. Och chi ddim gweld gola dydd o gwbwl tan yr 'af! Mae'n syndod bo' ni'n fyw, ondywe?

Well there was nothing else here, you see. Nothing. What else did you have? It was only the coal mine. You think about a young boy getting up at six o' clock in the morning, and going down to the pithead. And he was at work from half past six, you could say, until half past five or six o' clock at night. You didn't see daylight at all until summer! It's a wonder we're alive, isn't it?

Glöwr o Onllwyn, ganed 1887
Onllwyn miner, born 1887

Bachgen ifanc wrth ei waith yn un o byllau Rhondda, tua 1910
A young boy working underground, Rhondda, about 1910

8

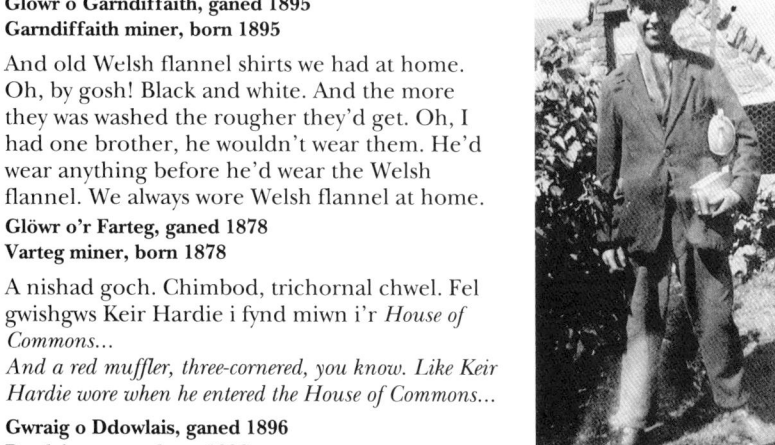

Gweithio ar y Glo *Working the Coal*

Swyddogion a gweithwyr ym Mhwll y Darren, y Deri, ger Bargoed, tua 1908
Officials and workmen at Darren Colliery, Deri, near Bargoed, about 1908

Stondin nwyddau gwlân ym marchnad Aberdâr, canol y 1920au
Woollen goods stall at Aberdare market, mid 1920s

Glöwr o Gilfach Goch, tua 1920
A Gilfach Goch collier, about 1920

Pair of working shoes, heavy nailed shoes and a moleskin trousers. You wasn't equipped unless you had your moleskin trousers on. And a pair of yorks - to tie around here look, on your trousers. Leather, like straps. And the idea of that was to stop the coal, rubbly coal, when you'd be using this box look, running down your trousers.
Glöwr o Garndiffaith, ganed 1895
Garndiffaith miner, born 1895

And old Welsh flannel shirts we had at home. Oh, by gosh! Black and white. And the more they was washed the rougher they'd get. Oh, I had one brother, he wouldn't wear them. He'd wear anything before he'd wear the Welsh flannel. We always wore Welsh flannel at home.
Glöwr o'r Farteg, ganed 1878
Varteg miner, born 1878

A nishad goch. Chimbod, trichornal chwel. Fel gwishgws Keir Hardie i fynd miwn i'r *House of Commons*...
And a red muffler, three-cornered, you know. Like Keir Hardie wore when he entered the House of Commons...
Gwraig o Ddowlais, ganed 1896
Dowlais woman, born 1896

Gweithio ar y Glo *Working the Coal*

Glowyr yn casglu eu lampiau, Glofa Oakdale, tua 1910
Colliers fetching their lamps, Oakdale Colliery, about 1910

Y papur lamp, odd yn rhaid i chi gâl y papur yna *'Please supply bearer with one safety lamp'*. A chwedi'ny, os na fydde'r papur 'na gyda chi i roi yn y *lamp room* y bore byddech chi'n dechre gweithio, bydde 'da chi ddim lamp i gâl. Ac hefyd och chi'n mynd lawr ar y *register* y foment och chi'n câl lamp. Ag on nw'n gwbod beth odd ych nymbar chi, a'n nymbar i odd "269". A fydde'r dyn fydde'n yr ystafell lampie 'ma, fydde fe'n mynd o gylch i gâl gweld pe bydde rai o'r lampie 'ma ddim wedi dod miwn yn y nos chwel. A pan fydde nw heb ddod miwn, wel wrth gwrs fydden nw'n chwilio amdanyn nw. Odd y lamp nawr fel ryw fath o leisens i chi i fod o dan ddaear.

The lamp paper, you had to have that piece of paper 'Please supply bearer with one safety lamp'. And if you didn't have that paper to hand into the lamp room on the morning you were starting work, you couldn't have a lamp. And you also went down on the register the moment you received your lamp. They knew your number, and my number was "269". And the man in the lamp room, he'd go round to look if some of the lamps weren't returned at night. When they didn't come back, of course, they'd go looking for them. That lamp was a kind of licence for you to be underground.

Glöwr o Bontyberem, ganed 1899
Pontyberem miner, born 1899

Glowyr yn cael mwgyn cyn mynd o dan ddaear, Glofa Pochin, tua 1910
Having a last cigarette before descending the pit, Pochin Colliery, about 1910

Gweithio ar y Glo *Working the Coal*

I was sixteen. I got on top of the Ocean pit, one of the fastest pits in Wales. I was put in the middle of the cage, and when the fellow pulled the grabs open, I was in the bottom of the pit. And my heart I think was coming out the back of my neck!
Glöwr o Hook, Penfro, ganed 1893
Miner from Hook, Pembrokeshire, born 1893

Fydda gynnoch chi stae ar y ffordd, yn 'r ha'. Odd pawb yn ista'n llygad am ryw funud ne ddau, ag och chi'n rhoi'ch pen i lawr fel hyn ynde, a siarad efo'ch gilydd. A chi'n sbïo fel hyn, a pen 'ddach chi ddechra 'nabod y bobol yn pasio, wel odd ych llygid chi'n dod at 'i hunin yn iawn ynde. Stae weld oddan ni'n galw honno. 'Dach weld wedi dod o'r haul yn y bore fedsach chi ddim gweld i lawr.

You'd have a rest on the way down, in the summer. Everybody would sit at the bottom of the pit for a minute or two - you'd put your head down like this and talk to one another. Then you'd look around, and when you could recognise the people passing, your eyes had become accustomed to the dark. We called that a stae weld *(lit. a break for seeing). You see, coming from the morning sun, you couldn't see anything.*
Glöwr ym Mhwll y Parlwr Du, ganed 1890
Miner at Point of Ayr Colliery, born 1890

Glowyr yn barod i fynd lawr y pwll, Glofa Oakdale, tua 1910
Colliers ready to descend, Oakdale Colliery, about 1910

Gwaelod y pwll, Glofa Lewis Merthyr, Trehafod, tua 1900
Pit bottom, Lewis Merthyr Colliery, Trehafod, about 1900

Gweithio ar y Glo *Working the Coal*

Drysau aer o dan ddaear, efallai yng Nglofa'r Bwllfa, Aberdâr, 1920au
Underground ventilation doors, possibly Bwllfa Colliery, Aberdare, 1920s

Gweithio wrth y ffas lo, De Cymru, 1930au
Working at the coalface, South Wales, 1930s

I went with my brother. He was working underground, and he took me with him. I went minding doors, but I was very nervous. Never experienced anything like it. And the horses used to be flying through with the trams. I'd open the door when they was coming and shut it after, owing to the ventilation. The ventilation had to go around a certain part of the workings for the men to work. Well, it frightened me as a boy, d'you see. And it was lonely by myself. I didn't like it. So my brother took me with him to work for a man that he was working for. And that's where I started on the coal first.
Glöwr o'r Farteg, ganed 1878
Dechreuodd weithio yn 11 oed
Varteg miner, born 1878
Started work at 11 years of age

The man at the coal face is the man digging the coal. So the more men they could get to the coal face and the less men they could get doing day work well the more profitable it was. See, that's understood. And everybody accepts that. Because further in it was going it meant more timber to support the roof - perhaps another engine to pull up - well the man that was driving the engine like myself wasn't doing anything to create the coal. I was just hauling the coal. My wages had to come from the man that was digging it.
Glöwr o Saundersfoot, Penfro, ganed 1902
Miner from Saundersfoot, Pembrokeshire, born 1902

Gweithio ar y Glo *Working the Coal*

Riparwyr wrth eu gwaith, efallai'n clirio cwymp o'r to, yng Nglofa Lewis Merthyr, tua 1910
Repairers at work, possibly clearing a roof fall, at Lewis Merthyr Colliery, about 1910

Sometimes you'd have eighteen inches of coal. Perhaps you'd have two foot or sometimes a bit more or a bit less. It varied. When you had a decent piece to work you could kneel down and cut it - well pretty good. But when you had to lie down on your side you couldn't produce so much then. I've seen a man one day - I was passing by and he was in under eleven inches. I looked up there and I could see this chap lying flat. Well I don't think I could get there, that I couldn't.
Glöwr o Saundersfoot, Penfro, ganed 1902
Miner from Saundersfoot, Pembrokeshire, born 1902

Well your hands would harden, do you see? And you had corns on your hands from using the tools. Oh yes. On the thumbs. Inside the thumbs from using the mandrel. Great big corns the size of a shilling, on some men's thumbs inside. From using the mandrels. Yes, digging under the coal and digging it up. 'Twas only of later years they got machines for breaking the coal up.
Glöwr o'r Farteg, ganed 1878
Varteg miner, born 1878

Amsar bo' chi'n iwso'r mandral a'r twls 'ma, odd ych dilo chi yn bollethi. Ta pryd och chi am fynd i neud dŵr, och chi'n neud dŵr yn ych dilo, yn golchi'ch dilo yn y dŵr 'yn. A odd 'wnnw'n neud llawar iawn o well'âd iddyn nw, yn gwella'r pollethi 'ma.

When you were using the mandrel and tools, you'd get blisters on your hands. Whenever you wanted to urinate, you'd do it on your hands, and wash your hands in the urine. And that made them a lot better, and cured these blisters.

Glöwr o Faesteg, ganed 1886
Maesteg miner, born 1886

13

Gweithio ar y Glo *Working the Coal*

Halio glo yng Nglofa Lewis Merthyr, tua 1900
Hauling coal at Lewis Merthyr Colliery, about 1900

Odd 'run faint o berygl gyta ceffyl dan ddaear â dyn chwel. A odd ceffyl yn gallu senso perygl o flân dyn cofiwch. Gwedwch chi bo' ceffyl yn sefyll acha hedin man'yn, a 'ta fa'n clŵad rwbath yn gwitho wrth 'i ben a, odd 'wnna'n gwichad fel plentyn. Odd a'n roi arwdd, yn gweu'thoch chi 'Shgwl, mwfa fi o man'yn cwic shgwl! Ma rwbath yn mynd i ddod lawr man'yn nawr!' Odd y sens 'na gita creatur.

A horse was in as much danger underground as a man. And a horse could sense danger before a man could. Say a horse was standing here at a heading, and he heard something working above him, it would squeal like a baby. It would give a sign, telling you 'Look, move me out of here quick! Something is going to come down here now!' The creature had that sense.

Glöwr o Gwmafan, ganed tua 1900
Cwmafan miner, born about 1900

Gweithio ar y Glo *Working the Coal*

Ma'n debig bod fi'n gywir wth ddeud bod 'na *ninety eight per cent* o goliars yn cnoi baco. Yn Balwr Du beth bynnag ynde. Achos oddach chi'n un hynod, os na 'ddach chi'n cnoi baco. Odd hyd yn oed y ceffyla yn cnoi baco! Odd ceffyla wth 'u bodd efo baco'n de. Ag oddan nw'n gwbod am y bobl rôi faco iddyn nhw hefyd. Peth arall hefyd odd y ceffyla'n neud odd isho llymad 'dach weld. Dal 'u tafoda allan ynde, a dyna fo. Ag oddan yn medru mynd i boceda bobol 'efyd a hôl y botal allan a'i dal o'i fyny - a'i yfad o i gyd! Yn amal iawn fyddach yn ffeindio ceg ych potal chi 'di câl 'i gwasgu. Potal dun ynde – oes 'na'm potela gwydyr i fod i lawr yn pwll.

I'm probably right in saying that ninety eight per cent of colliers used to chew tobacco. At Point of Ayr anyway. Because you were the exception if you didn't chew tobacco. Even the horses used to chew tobacco! They loved tobacco, and they knew who would give them some too. Another thing that the horses used to do was want a drink. They'd hang their tongues out and that was it. They could get into people's pockets, get the bottle out and drink it all! You'd very often find your bottle with its neck all squashed. It was a tin bottle, of course - glass bottles aren't allowed underground.

Glöwr ym Mhwll y Parlwr Du, ganed 1890
Miner at Point of Ayr Colliery, born 1890

Y ceffyl olaf i weithio yng Nglofa Bers, ger Wrecsam, 1952
The last pony to work at Bersham Colliery, near Wrexham, 1952

Gweithio ar y Glo *Working the Coal*

Llwytho dram yng Nglofa Lewis Merthyr, tua 1900
Filling a tram at Lewis Merthyr Colliery, about 1900

When we used to complain about the dust, the manager told us, 'What do you worry about, boy? You chew coal, it does you good. It cures heartburn, it'll cure chest troubles.' That was the short answer you had from the management.
Glöwr o Rymni, ganed 1881
Rhymni miner, born 1881

It was a terrible place for water. Oh lord, I have seen the water going in there, it was terrible... Well the water was coming down on them and they were lying in it like ducks. And the water was running in here through the neck of their shirts and it was running out through the leg of their trousers. In a river. Now there was a state on a man. It was so wet I've been coming home with a man on a frosty morning on a pushbike going across Kingsmoor Common - we had to come that way from Broome Colliery. This fellow was living in Saundersfoot and we'd be coming along pedalling - hard frost, freezing, and all of a sudden he'd topple one side and his leg would go to the ground. His trousers was frozen on his legs.
Glöwr o Saundersfoot, Penfro, ganed 1902
Miner from Saundersfoot, Pembrokeshire, born 1902

Gweithio ar y Glo *Working the Coal*

On nw'n mynd â bwyd i Pwll Dyffryn, yndifa. Odd llicod 'na. On nw 'run peth â *black pats* yn ritag bitu'r lle. A och chi'n goffo cario bwyd mewn bocs i gâl catw'r llicod mâs o'na. O diar diar! Odd neb yn mynd â bwyd dan ddaear mewn papur chwel. Miwn bocs, ne fydda'r llygotan yn myn' ato fe. Wath odd milodd o rai bach 'na chwel.

They used to take food with them to Dyffryn pit. There were mice there. They were just like black pats running about the place. And you had to carry your food in a box to keep the mice out of it. Oh dear, dear! No-one would take food underground wrapped in paper, see. In a box, or a mouse would get at it. There were thousands of them there.

Glöwr o Gwmafan, ganed tua 1900
Cwmafan miner, born about 1900

Os câch chi lwmp yn ych llygad oddan nw'n gyrru am Daff ne Dafydd Jones Tan Rhiw ynde, rhoi chi ar ych cefn ar lawr, a mi lyfa rownd ych llygad chi, cyn laned â'r aur i chi. Fyddach chi byth yn trwblo jist os bydda'n nw'n ymyl 'nde. Ond dach 'weld, oedd y tafod yn smŵdd iawn doedd? I fynd o gwmpas ych llygad chi. Odd isho dipyn o stwmog 'doedd?

If coal got in your eye, they'd send for Daff or Dafydd Jones Tan Rhiw, put you flat on your back on the floor, and he'd lick right round your eye, until it was as clean as gold. You weren't worried if they were about. But, you see, the tongue is very smooth, isn't it? To go around your eye. It needed a strong stomach, didn't it?

Glöwr ym Mhwll y Parlwr Du, ganed 1890
Miner at Point of Ayr Colliery, born 1890

Dau frawd yn cael seibiant ym Mhwll y Brithdir, Glofa'r Bargoed, tua 1920
Two brothers having a break at Brithdir Pit, Bargoed Colliery, about 1920

Gweithio ar y Glo *Working the Coal*

Glanio'r glo ar ben un o byllau'r Rhondda, tua 1913
Landing coal at the top of a Rhondda pit, about 1913

Then the coal then would be landed down here onto the screens - come up in the trams as you can imagine. Pulled out and weighed and tipped into big coal tips. Large coal - the next grade would be perhaps not so large and what you used to call it large coal and there was nuts, cobbles, beans and peas - you know. That was the grades, see. There used to be a revolving screen, you see, and the big coal lumps like that now would go over a screen and go out straight on to the tips. The small stuff that was left would go into a revolving screen and this screen was tapered and then there would be like a smaller mesh in the grid as they were going along. So it would keep rolling, rolling - you'd get a lump out perhaps that size. That would go down into a chute. And what was different that would go out. Peas was the last - a small one - well like your fingernail. And then the dust or the duff. It was sorted out then.

Glöwr o Saundersfoot, Penfro, ganed 1902
Miner from Saundersfoot, Pembrokeshire, born 1902

Y sgriniau, Glofa Bers, 1960au cynnar
Screens, Bersham Colliery, early 1960s

18

Gweithio ar y Glo *Working the Coal*

Casglu pai yng Nglofa'r Bwllfa, Aberdâr, 1920au
Collecting pay at Bwllfa Colliery, Aberdare, 1920s

12 cwt. of Coal to be supplied every four weeks to workmen who are householders, such coal to be consumed only on the premises occupied by those who are entitled to supplies.

EMLYN ANTHRACITE COLLIERY, LTD.
Week ending 20 FEB 1937 ....1937.

ASS. COLLIER.
ALBERT DAVIES,

Level	Yards	
Tophole		
Deep		
Slope		
Crossing		
Skip		
Stall		
Walling		
Double Turn		
Lower Side		
Ripping		
Allowance Each		
Level Timber		
Gears		
Toss		
T. Out		
Cogs		
Props		
Rubbish		
Cartage		
Days		
Minimum		
TOTAL		
Plus %		
Subsistance Wage		
TOTAL EARNINGS. £		

STOPPAGES.
Coal, Doctor, Insurance, Unemployment, Amb. & Hospital, Collections, Library, G. Insurance, Dr. Harper, Band, Blind Institute, Checks, Powder, Damages, Baths

Balance Due. £

Gweithio ar y Glo *Working the Coal*

Wy'n cofio y trains bysa'n paso man'yn pry'ny, chimbod. Odd train coliars yn paso - train dim ond i'r coliars. Och chi'n gwel' nw'n dod da thre bythdi'r tri o'r gloch ynifa, train coliars yn cyrradd y steishon man'yn. On nw'n dod yn un res o nw, chimbod - dinon du i gyd. Och chi'n meddwl bo' chi mâs yn y gwletydd pell...

I remember the trains that used to pass here then, you know. The colliers' train would pass by - a train only for the colliers. You'd see them come home about three o'clock, the colliers' train arriving at the station here. They'd come out in one line, you know, all black men. You'd think you were out in foreign parts.

Gwraig o Bont-rhyd-y-fen, ganed 1910
Pont-rhyd-y-fen woman, born 1910

Often, after we came home from work as collier's helpers, we used to fall to sleep over our dinner, because we were so exhausted. A boy of fourteen, fourteen and a half was expected to do the same work as his butty, who was a fully matured man, and one - we fell to sleep over dinner, and one had to face a bath afterwards. A zinc bath in front of the fireplace. The water was boiled on the hob in a bucket by the women of the house, and sometimes there were families of eight or nine working in the colliery. And they would bath their top half first and their bottom half after, from the senior member down. Usually the Dad, the eldest son down the line. The youngest son was always last.

Glöwr o Rymni, ganed 1881
Rhymni miner, born 1881

Ar ddiwedd y dydd, Wattstown, Rhondda, 1921
The end of the day, Wattstown, Rhondda

Glowyr gwaith Pochin ar y ffordd adref i Dredegar, tua 1910
Pochin colliers on the way home to Tredegar, about 1910

Gwaith y Ferch *A Woman's Work*

Y llun enwog o Mrs George, Pont-y-pŵl, yn golchi â thwb doli, tua 1900. Prin yw'r lluniau o waith tŷ yn y cyfnod hwn
The well-known photograph of Mrs George, Pontypool, washing with a dolly tub, about 1900. Photographs of domestic work during this period are rare

But it was hard for the mother where they was working in wet places. Awful mess on the working clothes d'you see. It'd dry and drop off round the house. See, old stone floors, see? And it was hard work for the woman

Glöwr o'r Farteg, ganed 1878
Varteg miner, born 1878

Odd lot o waith lle'r odd lot o fechgyn. Odd y merched yn goffo' gwitho'n galetach na'r bechgyn. Ar ôl iddyn nw ddod nôl odd y bechgyn yn batho o flân tân. Wel, allwch chi feddwl shwt le odd ar y gecin ar ôl 'ny, a'r merched weti'ny yn goffod golchi llawr y gecin. A gwaelod y trowseri falle wedi dod o'r gwaith yn botsh ishe golchi. 'Sa'r gard o flân y tân a llond y lle o drowseri yn sychu, yn barod i'r diwrnod ar ôl 'ny. Odd merched yn gorffod gwitho'n galed yr amser 'ny.

There was a lot of work where there were a lot of men. The women had to work harder than the men. After they'd come home, the men used to bath in front of the fire. Well, you can imagine the mess that was on the kitchen after that, and the women then had to wash the kitchen floor. And perhaps the bottom of their trousers coming from work would be in a mess needing washing. The guard in front of the fire would be full of trousers drying, ready for the following day. The women had to work hard in those days.

Gwraig o Resolfen, ganed 1902
Resolven woman, born 1902

Odd o'n cymryd trw'r dydd i olchi ers talwm. 'Chos odd 'i'n berwi dŵr yn y boilar yndoedd? Twb a doli a *rubbing board*. A wedyn os nag odd hi'n ddwrnod sychu allan, odd rhaid 'ddyn nw sychu'n tŷ yndoedd? Meddyliwch chi am goliars rwan a dillad budur. A 'wrach tyed o blant gynnyn nw hefyd.

It took all day to wash years ago. Because they had to boil water in a boiler, didn't they? A tub, a dolly and a rubbing board. And then if it wasn't a dry day, they'd have to dry indoors, didn't they? You think of colliers and their dirty clothes. And perhaps they'd have a houseful of children as well.

Gwraig o Rosllannerchrugog, ganed 1911
Miner's wife, Rhosllannerchrugog, born 1911

Strong soap, you know, and soda. Any amount of soda to boil them, innit? There was no other washing powders like they've got today. Nothing like that. No, soda. Handful of soda until your hands - there's no wonder we haven't got nice hands, innit?

Gwraig o Lwynypia, ganed 1895
Llwynypia miner's wife, born 1895

Gwaith y Ferch *A Woman's Work*

On ni'n gwitho'n galad. Ma nw wedi cintach roi arian i'r coliars - ddyla'r gwracidd i gæl dwybunt am olchu'u dillad nw. I fi gal gweu'thoch chi... Llinynnon gwyn ar y drofersi. A tu fiwn i'r copish felna. A reina'n cal 'u scrwbo 'da scrwbin brwsh. Fel yr eira gwyn. 'Sen nw ddim ond dou ddiwrnod yn y gwaith cyn bo nw'n ddu fel y pentan. Ond 'na fe on nw'n myn' yn læn.

We worked hard. They've grumbled about giving money to the colliers - the wives ought to get £2 for washing their clothes! There were white strings in the underpants, and inside the fly like that. They were scrubbed with a scrubbing brush. They were like the driven snow. After only two days in work, they were as black as the hob, but at least they went out clean.

Gwraig o Ddowlais, ganed 1896
Miner's wife, Dowlais Top, born 1896

Odd menŵod yn llefan amser och chi'n dod â trowsus gwaith sha thre iddyn nw chwel, wath nawr rint bod y 'wys chwel a'r cwbwl, odd a'n mynd fel 'arn chwel, mynd fel 'arn. On nw'n gorffod patsho fe yndifa, rhoi pishyn arno fa. 'Sach chi'n gweld twmpe mawr o sebon wrth 'u ochor nw, pwsho'r notwdd miwn i'r sebon gynta chwel, a goffod câl notwdd gryf ato fe 'ed.

Women used to cry when you brought working trousers home to them, because with the sweat and everything, they'd get as hard as iron. They had to patch them, didn't they? You'd see great lumps of soap by the side of them - they'd push the needle into the soap first. And they had to have a strong needle to do the job as well.

Glöwr o Ddowlais, ganed 1893
Dowlais miner, born 1893

Dau lŵr o Gwmaman wedi dychwelyd o'u gwaith yng Nglofa Cwmneol, 1939
Two Cwmaman miners after returning home from work at Cwmneol Colliery, 1939

Gwaith y Ferch *A Woman's Work*

Teulu o Donyrefail, tua 1890

A Tonyrefail family, about 1890

Morwmon odd y merched yn câl mynd. Ne gwetwch chi bod lot o dulu, odd y ferch 'ena'n goffo bod yn tŷ, i 'elpu'r fam. Odd dim dewish 'ta'r ferch 'ena. A'dd lot yn mynd rown i olchi weti'ny. A gwinio. Gwetwch nawr bo' gwinyddas a bo' chi 'di pyrnu denfydd, wel och chi'n mynd i'r tŷ 'yn am falla tri diwarnod, dim ond i winio i'r tulu 'na chwel. A cario'u mashins 'da nw cofiwch.

The girls went to work as maids. Or if they were a large family, the eldest daughter had to stay at home, to help the mother. The eldest daughter had no choice. And some would go out washing. Or sewing. Say now there was a seamstress and you'd bought some material - well, you'd go to that house for perhaps three days, only to sew for that family. And they carried their machines with them mind.

Gwraig o Bont-rhyd-y-fen, ganed 1910
Pont-rhyd-y-fen woman, born 1910

Gwaith y Ferch *A Woman's Work*

Siop nwyddau llaethdy ym Mhen-y-graig, 1914
Shop selling dairy produce in Pen-y-graig, 1914

(It was) only a parlour shop. You'd be surprised what she kept there. And what she cooked. My father's health broke down, d'you see, and she just had to do something, you know. And that's the way she kept going. Talk about smells, they were gorgeous, because she cooked everything. She sold all kinds of sweets - like a kind a tuck shop, you know. She also sold butter and biscuits and cooked meats. But the most of the cooking was done herself. I think it maybe broke my mother's heart to give up her sitting room, but I mean, she coped. Because we didn't get unemployment or sick pay in those years, you see.

Gwraig o Gwm Ogwr, ganed 1905
Ogmore Vale woman, born 1905

Gwraig yn cario babi "Welsh fashion", Rhondda, 1930au
Woman carrying a baby "Welsh fashion", Rhondda, 1930

We had a good clean home, you know, - good mother, and I mean a careful mother. Not a drunkard nor nothing like that. My father used to like a little drop mind, I'm not saying... And the only outing we used to go on was with the Sunday school. We'd go to Porthcawl. We'd walk to Pen-y-graig station, I'd have a couple of coppers, and that's all we had to be satisfied. Take our own food innit? And that's all my mother ever went, love 'er.

Gwraig o Lwynypia, ganed 1895
Llwynypia woman, born 1895

Bywyd Cymdeithasol *Social Life*

Glowyr y tu allan i'r Miners Arms, Pwll-y-glaw, 1920au
Colliers outside the Miners Arms, Pwll-y-glaw, 1920s

Now I recall that when I started work I was given a four pint jack, and filled with water. And my father said, 'A pinch of salt, boy.' 'Why Dad?' 'Well, when you perspire, all the salts come out of your body with the perspiration. Make them up, good lad, and you'll always be strong.' Now an amusing incident here is that the old - I'll call them alcoholics in the lighter sense - they used to say to drink eight or ten pints of beer nightly. And that was a good cure for perspiration, to make up the lost fluids of the body and also to flush the liver out. But on the other hand, the chapel people used to maintain that if you had dirty dishes or dirty clothes, you would not wash them in a pint of beer! You'd wash them in hot or cold water, which I thought was a good point.
Glöwr o Rymni, ganed 1881
Rhymni miner, born 1881

Welas rai, cofiwch, yn swilo'u gena o'r cwrw, chi'n diall, a'i boeri allan. A rai eraill wet'ny yn citsho'n y peint a lan â fe i gyd. A weti'ny odd 'na lot o garthu, a'dd *spittoons* a bwceti abythdi'r lle iddyn nw boeri yndo fa, ar ôl y peint cynta.

I saw some, mind, swilling their mouths with the beer and spitting it out. And others then grabbing the pint and downing it all. Then there'd be a lot of clearing of the throat, and there were spittoons and buckets about the place for them to spit into, after that first pint.
Glöwr o Faesteg, ganed 1886
Maesteg miner, born 1886

They used to meet on a weekend and have a drink together. And very often a sing-song. Mind, the men in those days, in the pubs, they used to have an enjoyable time. They'd have the piano going, and singing old songs.
Glöwr o'r Farteg, ganed 1878
Varteg miner, born 1878

Y Colliers Arms, Craig-cefn-parc, ddiwedd y 19eg ganrif
The Colliers Arms, Craig-cefn-parc, late 19th century

25

Bywyd Cymdeithasol *Social Life*

Glowyr yn mwynhau eu diod yng Nghwm-bach, Aberdâr, tua 1910
Colliers enjoying a drink in Cwm-bach, Aberdare, about 1910

Wi'n cofio'r amser odd 'i ddim yn sâff iawn i chi fod mâs ar yr hewl bythdi ddeg ar gloch nos Satwn. Wath fydda ymladd ofnadw wastod chwel. Odd 'i ddim yn câl 'i 'styried yn neis bo' merch mâs yr amser 'ny.

I remember a time when it wasn't very safe for you to be out on the street about ten o' clock on a Saturday night. Because there'd always be an awful lot of fighting, you see. It wasn't considered nice for a woman to be out at that time.

Gwraig o Resolfen, ganed 1902
Resolven woman, born 1902

Odd ddim merch cal myn' i dafarn. Dele'i ddim miwn - cele'i ddim myn' miwn. Dim ond i'r *snug* on nw'n câl mynd. Och chi ddim fod i gymysgu, dinon a menŵod miwn tafarn. Duw! Bydda Mam 'di'n lladd ni 'ta ni'n mynd i dŷ menyw odd yn ifed. 'Paid a neud 'na 'to cofia! Paid di â myn 'da'r fenyw 'na, ma 'onna'n ifed cofia!' Odd ddim menŵod yn myn' i dafarn, 'na fe. Och chi'n gomon. Edrych arnoch chi. Allech chi ddim myn' i cwrdd. O Duw! Sôn amdanoch chi, y sawl odd yn myn' i'r cwrdd.

They wouldn't allow a girl to go into a pub. She wouldn't come in - she wasn't allowed to come in. She could only go as far as the snug. You weren't supposed to mix, men and women in a pub. Good grief, Mam would have killed us if we went to the house of a woman who drank. 'Don't do that again mind! Don't go to that woman's house. She drinks, you know!' Women didn't go to pubs, and that was that. You were common. People looked at you. You couldn't go to chapel. Good grief, they'd talk about you, those that went to chapel.

Gŵr o Dreforys, ganed 1913
Morriston man, born 1913

Bywyd Cymdeithasol *Social Life*

Agoriad Capel Ebenezer, Y Maerdy, 1912
Opening Ebenezer Chapel, Mardy, 1912

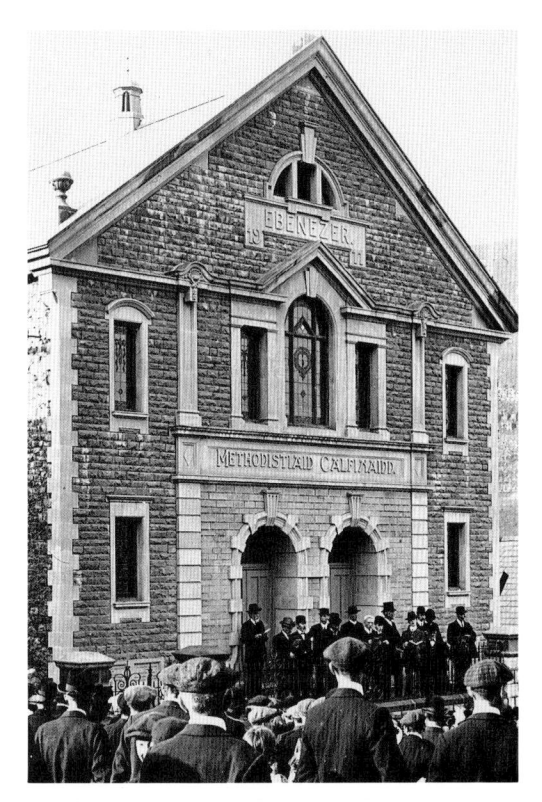

Band of Hope plwyf Abercynon: perfformwyr y *Fairy Ring*, 1921
Parish of Abercynon Band of Hope: the cast of the Fairy Ring, *1921*

All our social life was all with the chapel. Because there was something there every night of the week for us. Either little plays, or there'd be children's operettas. Or the big choir then, we'd have the cantatas. And there'd be Young People's Society and *Cwrdd Gweddi* as we'd call it. Prayer meeting on a Monday night. And then there was *Gyfeillach* as we used to call it on Thursday night. Oh, it used to be years ago, we were over 300 members in this little church here. In our chapel. Even the gallery and all used to be full there. Everybody went to chapel then. That was our way of life. Our social life was all around the church. And it wasn't dull, mind. We had an awful lot of fun.
Gwraig o Lwynypia, ganed 1904
Llwynypia woman, born 1904

Och chi'n cystadlu yn y *Band of Hope* amser honno. Ag on ni'n trio mynd i *Band of Hope*, pawb, yndoedd? 'Sech chi'n adrodd yn dda, ddim yn anghofio, chi'n câl ceniog, a odd nene'n werthfawr yndoedd? O' 'ne *Band of Hope* i bob capel. Ac wir, odd o'n dda yn mynd i *Band of Hope*. Canu a dysgu adrodd, a un a'r llall yn siarad. O! odd *Band of Hope* yn le gwerth mynd iddo.

You used to compete in the Band of Hope in those days. We would all try to go to the Band of Hope, wouldn't we? If you recited well, and didn't forget, you'd get a penny, and that was valuable wasn't it? There was a Band of Hope for each chapel. And it was really good. Singing and learning to recite, and people talking. Oh! the Band of Hope was a place worth going to.
Gwraig o Rosllannerchrugog, ganed 1911
Rhosllannerchrugog woman, born 1911

Bywyd Cymdeithasol *Social Life*

Gorymdaith Ysgolion Sul ar hyd Stryd Morgan, Tredegar, tua 1910
A Sunday School Parade down Morgan Street, Tredegar, about 1910

Bora Dy' Llun Sulgwyn bydde'r ysgolion yn troi mâs chwel. A'r band, band y lle. On ni'n meddwl bod 'wnna'n *thrill* chimod, yn cerad trw'r lle a'r band yn wara'r tona i ni, a ni'n martsho!

Whit Monday, all the (Sunday) schools would turn out. And the band, the local band. We used to think that was a thrill, you know, walking through the village with the band playing the tunes, and us marching!

Gwraig o Bont-rhyd-y-fen, ganed 1905
Pont-rhyd-y-fen woman, born 1905

Martsho Llungwyn chwel. *Turn out* yr ysgolion Sul i gyd. Wy'n cofio, sgitshe bach gwyn 'da'r merched i gyd, a'r ffrils a'r ffrals. Odd câ wetyn yn cal i ddoti mâs chwel, a odd stondings ar y câ chwel, gwerthu taffis a *oranges* a fale falle, a wedyn 'se grŵp fan hyn a grŵp fan 'na, 'se rheina yn ware *twos and threes* a *kissing ring* myn' lan fel 'yn. Rasys wedyn chimod, ennill dime.

We'd march on Whit Monday. All the Sunday schools would turn out. I remember all the girls had little white shoes, and the frills and the fralls. A field was laid out with stalls selling sweets and oranges and maybe apples, and there'd be a group here and a group there - They'd play twos and threes and kissing ring. And then they'd have races, for a halfpenny prize.

Gwraig o Resolfen, ganed 1902
Resolven woman, born 1902

Bywyd Cymdeithasol *Social Life*

Y Trip Ysgol Sul, wel odd 'wnna'r *highlight* y flwyddyn. Porthcawl. On ni'n mynd 'da'r train chwel. Odd Sardis pen pella'r pentra, a capel Methodist Jerusalem, a Bethal capel y Bedyddwyr yn uno, a'n nw'n câl train wetyn chwel. Pawb yn mynd i Borthcawl ar yr un diwyrnod. Cwrs odd 'wnna'n neud a'n well byth! Ow! On i'n mynd mor *excited* odd stumog tost 'ta fi bob bora 'sa'r trip. A mynd grôs y Bont a gweld pawb yn mynd - *pawb* yn mynd. Wel! On ni blant yn wyllt! A miwn i'r train, a pan on ni wrth Tai Isha, on ni gyd nawr, Mam yn gweu'thon ni 'Drychwch mâs fan'yn nawr.' Achos 'na'r unig rai odd ar ôl yn Oakwood i gyd yr ochor 'yn i'r Bont, yr unig ddwy odd ar ôl o bawb odd Bopa a Mary Jane. 'Na'r *orders* – 'Drychwch mâs nawr ar Bopa a Mary Jane.' A'dd Bopa a Mary Jane wedi cerad lawr wrth y clwydi, ag yn wafo fel 'ta ni'n myn' i *Australia* chimod. A ni blant i gyd yn wafo nes bo nw'ch dwy mâs o'r golwg.

The Sunday School Trip was the highlight of the year. Porthcawl. We'd go by train, see. Sardis at the far end of the village, Jerusalem the Methodist chapel, and Bethel the Baptist chapel would join up and get a train. Everybody going to Porthcawl on the same day. Of course that made it even better! Oh, I'd get so excited that I always had a stomach ache on the morning of the trip. And we'd cross the bridge and see everybody going, everybody going. Well, we kids would go wild! Then into the train, and when we got to Tai Isha, Mam would tell us 'Look out by 'ere now.' Because the only people left in the whole of Oakwood this side of the bridge, the only two left were Bopa and Mary Jane. Those were the orders, 'Look out for Bopa and Mary Jane now.' And Bopa and Mary Jane would have walked down as far as the gates, and they'd wave as if we were going to Australia. And we kids would wave back at them until they both disappeared from sight.

Gwraig o Bont-rhyd-y-fen, ganed 1925
Pont-rhyd-y-fen woman, born 1925

Trip Capel Bethann, Bryncethin, i Borthcawl, tua 1910
Outing of Bethann Chapel, Bryncethin, to Porthcawl, about 1910

TABERNACLE BAPTIST CHAPEL, PONTYPOOL.

THE ANNUAL TEA PARTY

OF THE ABOVE CHURCH WILL BE HELD

On Thursday, August the 29th, 1872;
Tea on the Table at Three o'clock. Tickets, 1s. each.

If the weather is favourable, the Tea will be provided in Penygarn Field— if wet, in the Tabernacle Chapel.

A PUBLIC MEETING
AT SEVEN O'CLOCK.

H. HUGHES, PRINTER, BOOKBINDER, AND STATIONER, COMMERCIAL STREET, PONTYPOOL.

Bywyd Cymdeithasol *Social Life*

Band Pres Ystradgynlais 1905. Rhwng 1903 a 1904, enillasant 18 o wobrau
Ystradgynlais Prize Band, 1905. Winners of 18 prizes in the years 1903 and 1904

Fe godwd yr *Hall* yn y pentra 'ma wedi'r Ryfal Ginta. A 'na le odd y bois i gyd yn mynd 'na yn y nos. Odd dwy ford *billiards* 'na. Odd rwbath yn myn' mlân 'na jest bob nos. Achos och chi'n câl practis opera ar nos Lun a nos Iau, weti'ny bydda'r *Male Voice* fach 'na, we'ny'r cwmni drama. Och chi'n meddwl yn amal odd dim dicon o nosweithi yn yr wthnos!

The Hall in the village was raised after the First World War. And that's where the boys would go in the evening. There were two billiard tables there. And there was something on every night. Because you'd have opera practice on the Monday and Thursday night, then there was the Male Voice party, then the drama company. You often felt there wasn't enough nights in the week!

Gŵr o Bont-rhyd-y-fen, ganed 1908
Pont-rhyd-y-fen man, born 1908

Mid Rhondda was a hot bed of singing. Now really good class singers came from this locality. And choirs. Because the old Mid Rhondda choir was about 250 strong. Now they can't keep a choir going here - a mixed choir. The only choirs in the valley now really are male voice choirs. I think people are more inclined now, if they want to hear something, they go down to St. David's Hall like, see, and pay five or six quid for it. But there you are. That's modern times, innit?

Gŵr o Donypandy, ganed 1906
Tonypandy man, born 1906

Côr Unedig Dowlais mewn cyngerdd yn Neuadd y Frenhines, 1936
The Dowlais United Choir at a concert in the Queen's Hall, London, 1936.

Bywyd Cymdeithasol *Social Life*

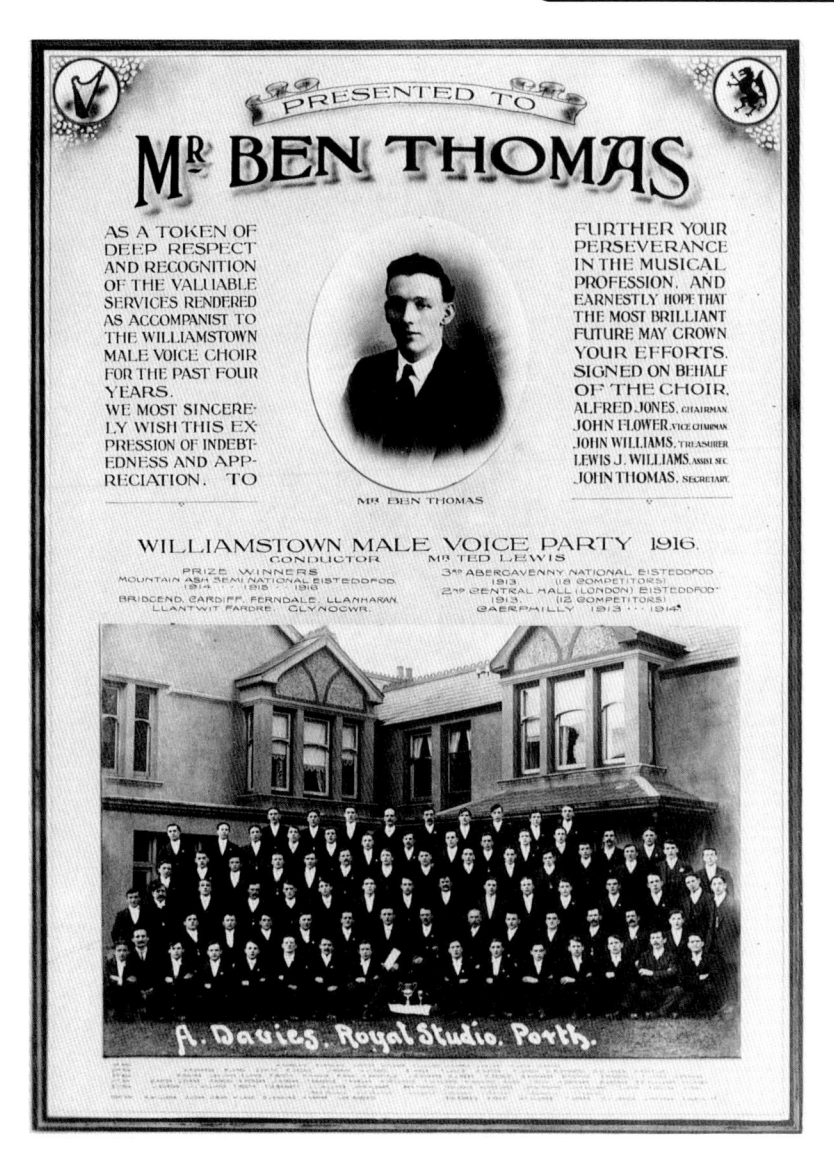

PRESENTED TO
Mr BEN THOMAS

AS A TOKEN OF DEEP RESPECT AND RECOGNITION OF THE VALUABLE SERVICES RENDERED AS ACCOMPANIST TO THE WILLIAMSTOWN MALE VOICE CHOIR FOR THE PAST FOUR YEARS. WE MOST SINCERELY WISH THIS EXPRESSION OF INDEBTEDNESS AND APPRECIATION TO FURTHER YOUR PERSEVERANCE IN THE MUSICAL PROFESSION, AND EARNESTLY HOPE THAT THE MOST BRILLIANT FUTURE MAY CROWN YOUR EFFORTS. SIGNED ON BEHALF OF THE CHOIR.
ALFRED JONES, CHAIRMAN
JOHN FLOWER, VICE CHAIRMAN
JOHN WILLIAMS, TREASURER
LEWIS J. WILLIAMS, ASST. SEC.
JOHN THOMAS, SECRETARY.

Mr BEN THOMAS

WILLIAMSTOWN MALE VOICE PARTY 1916
CONDUCTOR Mr TED LEWIS
PRIZE WINNERS
MOUNTAIN ASH SEMI NATIONAL EISTEDDFOD 1914 - 1915 - 1916
BRIDGEND, CARDIFF, FERNDALE, LLANHARAN, LLANTWIT FARDRE, GLYNOGWR.
3rd ABERGAVENNY NATIONAL EISTEDDFOD 1913 (18 COMPETITORS)
2nd CENTRAL HALL (LONDON) EISTEDDFOD 1913 (12 COMPETITORS)
CAERPHILLY 1913 ... 1914.

A. Davies, Royal Studio, Porth.

Dy' Sul a Dy' Llun, Dy' Mawrth, Dy' Mercher a nos Wener, *Male Voice* – myn i rihyrsal *Male Voice* a'r capeli. A yn y gaea chwel, trw'r gaea odd yr *oratorios* yn disgi Meseia a rina. Wedyn odd reina yn darfod, gwedwch *June July*. Wel odd y bechgyn 'na i gyd wedi'ny'n mynd i'r Orpheus i'r *National*. On' na'r byw chwel. Ŵ! Odd e'n grêt! On ni'n gweld ni'n mynd i *North Wales* i'r Bala - naw *bus*. Naw *bus* cofiwch! Gwedwch bod y côr yn cymeryd tair *bus*, odd wech arall yn ffrindie'n dod 'ta ni. Neud trip. On nw'n mynd acha bore Dy' Gwener i *North Wales*, nôl nos Sul. Duw, odd e'n *event!* Wel odd dim Costa del Sol a pethe fel'ny! Canu ar y Crôs weti'ny. 'Tach chi un, dou tri ar gloch y bore, odd canu ar y Crôs. Pawb mâs. Odd y Crôs yn ddu! Odd 'na gannodd ar y Crôs yn aros i'r côr ddod nôl o *North Wales*. A hyd yn ôd pan odd steddfode bach fel Treorci, Ammanford, Bridgend, Clunderwen - odd bown o fod cwrdda ar y Crôs, a *time* bach o Gymanfa Ganu wedi'ny sbo'r bore chwel. Wel 'na'r byw, chwel. Odd pawb â rywun 'da nw'n perthyn yn y côr. Odd e'n *event!*

Sunday, Monday, Tuesday, Wednesday and Friday night, it was the Male Voice - we went to Male Voice rehearsals and the chapels. And in the winter, throughout the winter there were the oratorios - learning the Messiah and all that. Then they'd come to an end say in June, July. Well, those boys then would all go to the Orpheus for the National. That was the way of life. Oh, it was great! I've seen us go to North Wales to Bala - nine buses. Nine buses mind! Say the choir was taking up three buses, there were six more for our supporters. Muking a trip of it. They'd go on a Friday night to North Wales and come back on Sunday night. It was an event. Well there wasn't anything like the Costa del Sol in those days. Then there'd be singing on Morriston Cross. Even if it was one, two, three o' clock in the morning, there'd be singing on the Cross. Everybody was out. The Cross would be black (with people). There were hundreds waiting for the choir to come back from North Wales. And even when there were smaller eisteddfodau like Treorchy, Ammanford, Bridgend, Clunderwen - there had to be a reception on the Cross, and then a little bit of a Gymanfa Ganu until morning. Well that was the way of life. Everybody had someone related to them in the choir. It was an event!

Gŵr o Dreforys, ganed 1913
Morriston man, born 1913

31

Bywyd Cymdeithasol *Social Life*

Theatr yr Empire, Stryd Dunraven, Tonypandy, tua 1912
Empire Theatre, Dunraven Street, Tonypandy, about 1912

On ni'n mynd i'r *films* ddwywaith yr wthnos. I Shew Sam on ni'n myn' fwya, yn Brynaman. Odd dim enw arall - Shew Sam odd e'n gâl mynd 'da pawb. On ni'n myn' lawr i Shew Sam a gâl *thruppenny* ticket. Ond gyda odd y gole'n mynd mâs, ôn ni fynycha yn mynd lawr dros ben y *board* i'r *fourpenny* seats. On ni'n gâl sbri ofnadw bo' ni'n gallu neud 'na!

We went to the films twice a week. We usually went to 'Shew Sam' (Sam's Show), in Brynaman. It didn't have another name - it was known by everyone as 'Shew Sam'. We'd buy thruppenny tickets, but once the light went out, we'd usually go over the top of the board to the fourpenny seats. We had a lot of fun doing that!

Gŵr o Lanaman, ganed 1910
Glanaman man, born 1910

I always remember the cinemas. We used to go down the Regal, you know - forms to sit down, no back or nothing to them, you know. We would queue up to sit in the front so that we could lean on the - what would you call it - not balustrade - we used to lean on that, you see? And again if you weren't there early enough, people would have hats on, and somebody would shout, 'Hey! Take your hat off! We can't see!'

Gwraig o Dreforys, ganed 1910
Morriston woman, born 1910

Dillad diwetydd a dillad dy' Sul. Odd dillad a dim ond Dy' Sul odd reina i fod. Wath wi'n cofio fi'n mynd - 'Wel shgwl, ma'r 'en siwt fach 'na tipyn bach yn *shabby*. Cer â dillad gore heno nawr i'r Globe. A er mwyn y mawredd, newita nw pan dywi di nôl streit, lle bo' dy dad-cu yn gweld nw. Wath O! Fydde'n gweud bo' ti mynd â siwt yr Ysbryd Glân at y diafol!'

There were evening clothes and Sunday clothes. Some clothes you could only wear on a Sunday. Because I remember when I went - 'Well look now, this suit has gone a bit shabby. Wear your best clothes tonight to the Globe. But for God's sake, change straight away when you get back, before your grandfather sees you. Because Oh! He'll say that you're taking the Holy Spirit's suit to the devil!'

Gŵr o Graig-cefn-parc, ganed 1905
Craig-cefn-parc man, born 1905

Bywyd Cymdeithasol *Social Life*

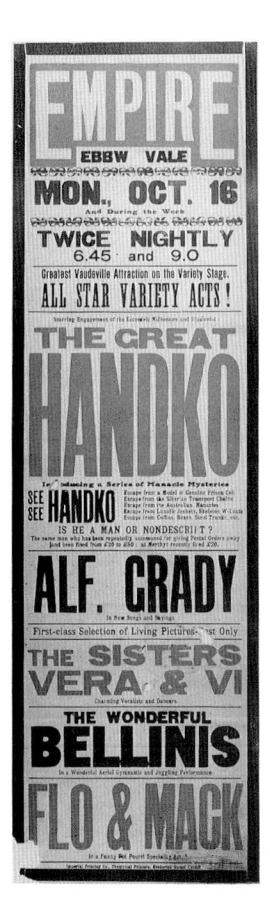

Wi'n cofio mynd lawr i'r Gnoll yn dre i'r picshwrs. A rint y picshwrs odd *variety* - rywun yn wara piano ne canu ne rwpath felna. Ond *silent* of cwrs. Wi'n cofio'r *talkies* cynta'n dod - Al Johnson ife? Sonny Boy.

I remember going to the Gnoll in town to the pictures. And between the films there was variety - someone playing piano or singing or something like that. But silent (films) of course. I remember the first talkies coming - Al Johnson is it? Sonny Boy.

Gwraig o Resolfen, ganed 1902
Resolven woman, born 1902

Everything was timed on our music, you see? Each member of the orchestra had it timed. But the main thing was to follow the head violinist, or sometimes it was the conductor. Perhaps it'd be cowboys now, and you'd have very quick music and all that business. Well you'd perhaps repeat that section four times. You couldn't rely on what you had in your music. You had to keep your eye now on the conductor, simply because the operator would go faster, and he shouldn't. Well after that, perhaps somebody'd be dying, somebody'd fall off a horse. Well now, 'twas no good us playing fast music when this person would be dead, you see? It was really funny, mind. Uncle Sid was to the second! He had his eye up there - wonderful memory for music - he'd look up - Right, he's fallen off! And he was accurate!

Gwraig o Dreforys, ganed 1910, a oedd yn aelod o deulu a fyddai'n ennill eu bywoliaeth trwy ganu offerynnau llinynnol yn sinemâu a chapeli'r cylch, yng nghyfnod y ffilmiau mud a'r cyngherddau mawreddog.

Cellist from Morriston, born 1910. Her father and uncle were also string musicians. As a family they earned their living playing in cinemas during the silent film era and also in chapel concerts and oratorios.

Bywyd Cymdeithasol *Social Life*

Institiwt y Gweithwyr, Blaenafon, ar ddechrau'r ganrif
Blaenavon Workmen's Institute, early this century

Institiwt y Glowyr, Cefncribwr, tua 1920
Cefn Cribbwr Miners' Institute, about 1920

THE LEWIS MERTHYR COLLIERIES WORKMEN'S HALL AND INSTITUTE

BY-LAWS

Name.

1. The name of the Institute shall be The Lewis Merthyr Collieries Workmen's Hall and Institute.

Qualification for Membership.

2. Any person employed in or about coal mines including in particular any person employed at the Lewis Merthyr Colliery who is willing to pay the subscription and any inhabitants of Porth or the surrounding neighbourhood who undertakes to pay his subscription may apply to become a member.

Admision of Members.

3. (a) Every candidate for admission as a Member shall submit his name and address to the Committee together with an undertaking that he will, if admitted, allow deduction from his wages, or, as the case may be, pay instalments of subscriptions for at least six months and the

Bywyd Cymdeithasol *Social Life*

Yn Resolfen nawr odd *Reading Room* chi'n gwel'. Odd lot o ddadla. Odd y *Reading Room* - wel, allwch chi weud taw *House of Commons* y lle odd a chwel. A wi'n cofio'r wireless cynta'n dod weti'ny. Lan i'r *Reading Room* dâth e. A wetyn odd menywod yn câl myn' miwn i wrando ar y *wireless* am y tro cynta. Odd e'n nosweth bwysig iawn!

In Resolven now there was a Reading Room, you see. There was a lot of debating. You could say that the Reading Room was the House of Commons of the village. And I remember the first wireless coming. It came to the Reading Room. And women were allowed in to listen to the wireless for the first time. It was a very important evening!

Gwraig o Resolfen, ganed 1902
Resolven woman, born 1902

We got a tutor to teach us Industrial History because we thought, well, there's something wrong here and we wanted to know the reason why. And we carried on with these classes until the strike of 1926. I left school at 11, and in this adult school we didn't have no strangers to lecture, it was just the members of the class. We had the Treherbert schoolmaster as the leader. And he said one Sunday - I'd never written a paper in my life, and he said one Sunday, 'Mr Thomas Blaen-cwm will give us a paper on the Renaissance next Sunday.' Well that knocked me for six, because I didn't know the meaning of the word renaissance! And I took all that week and a bit of help from other people and I wrote a paper anyway. And I've been looking out the history of the Renaissance, and I've got it pretty well.

Glöwr o Flaen-cwm, ganed tua 1890
Blaen-cwm miner, born around 1890

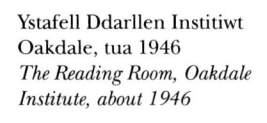

Ystafell Ddarllen Institiwt Oakdale, tua 1946
The Reading Room, Oakdale Institute, about 1946

Dyddiau Blin *Hard Times*

In Loving Memory
OF THE
MINERS WHO LOST THEIR LIVES
— IN —
WELSH COLLIERY DISASTERS

	Killed.		Killed.
1934—September 22, Gresford, Wrexham	261	1878—September 1, Abercarn	62
1932—January 25, Llwynypia, Rhondda	11	1877—March 8, Worcester Pit, Swansea	18
1931—Aug. 25, Caerau, Mountain Out-crop	3	1876—December 13, Abertillery	20
1929—July 10, Milfraen, Blaenavon	9	1875—December 5, Llan Pit, Pentyrch	12
1929—Nov. 28, Wernbwll, nr. Penclawdd	7	1875—December 4, New Tredegar	22
1927—March 1, Cwm, Ebbw Vale	52	1874—July 24, Charles Pit, Llansamlet	19
1923—April 26th, Trimsaran	9	1874—April 5, Abertillery	6
1913—October 13, Senghenydd	436	1872—March 8, Wernfach	18
1905—July 5, Wattstown	119	1872—March 2, Victoria	19
1905—March 10, Clydach Vale	31	1872—Jan. 10, Oakwood, Llynvi Valley	11
1901—September 10, Llanbradach	12	1871—October 4, Gelli Pit, Aberdare	4
1901—May 24, Senghenydd	82	1871—February 24, Pentre	38
1899—August 18, Llest Colliery, Garw	19	1870—July 23, Llansamlet	19
1896—January 28, Tylorstown	57	1869—June 10, Ferndale	60
1894—June 25, Cilfynydd	276	1869—May 23, Llanerch	7
1892—August 26, Park Slip	110	1867—November 8, Ferndale	178
1892—Aug. 12, Great Western Colliery	58	1865—December 20, Upper Gethin	30
1890—March 8, Morfa	87	1865—June 16, Tredegar	2
1890—February 6, Llanerch	176	1863—December 24, Maesteg	14
1890—January 20, Glyn Pit, Pontypool	5	1863—October 17, Margam	39
1888—May 14, Aber, Tynewydd	5	1862—February 19, Gethin, Merthyr	47
1887—February 18, Ynyshir	37	1860—December 1, Risca	146
1885—December 24, Mardy	81	1859—April 5, Neath Chain Colliery	26
1885—Naval Colliery	14	1858—October 13, Duffryn	20
1884—Nov. 8, Pochin Colliery, Tredegar	14	1856—July 13, Cymmer	114
1884—January 28, Penygraig	11	1853—March 12, Risca Vale	10
1884—January 16, Cwmavon	10	1852—May 10, Duffryn	64
1883—August 21, Gelli	4	1850—Dec. 14, New Duffryn Colliery	13
1883—February 1, Coedcae	5	1849—Aug. 11, Lletty Shenkin, Aberdare	52
1883—February 11, Coedcae	6	1848—June 21, Victoria (Mon.)	11
1882—January 15, Risca	4	1846—January 14, Risca	35
1880—Dec. 10, Naval Steam Colliery	96	1845—August 2, Cwmbach	28
1880—July 15, Risca	119	1844—January 1, Dinas	12
1879—Sept. 22, Waunllwyd, Ebbw Vale	84	1837—June 17, Blaina (Mon.)	21
1879—January 13, Dinas	3	1837—May 10, Plas-yr-Argoed, Mold	21
1878—September 11, Abercarn	268		

"IN THE MIDST OF LIFE WE ARE IN DEATH."
Let's hope the Gallant Miners havn't died in vain,
On God's own shore their friends might meet them once again.

C. P., TR.

One was a very popular song - Don't go down in the mines, Daddy. Now there was several explosions about. I was about ten year old when a big explosion happened just down the valley here. A hundred and seventy-six was killed. All down through the valley here the blinds was drawn. I went for a walk down with my brother - blinds was down. Families, four boys and a father in one house wiped out. It's a terrible thing the explosion. It would rip solid rock down, and buckle steel drams up like a piece of lead. Terrible. And sometimes fires would break out, d'you see? If there was much dust. Oh I remember it...
Glöwr o'r Farteg, ganed 1878
Varteg miner, born 1878

Fe glŵas i bod *explosion* wedi bod ar y Bryn, ag on i ddim gwpod pwy. Ond wedi i fi ddod da thre, fe geso'i wbod mai 'y mrawd i odd un o nw a 'mrawd yng ngyfreth a bachan arall. Mi es i'r *hospital* i' gwel' nw'n y gwely. O! 'Na'r olygfa ryfedda! Odd yr *explosion* wedi wthu'r glo miwn iddi crôn nw, chimbod. Odd 'u gwynepa nw gwmws 'run peth â cnepyn o lo.

I'd heard that there'd been an explosion at Bryn, and I didn't know who. But once I got home, I found out that my brother was one of them, and my brother in law and another man. I went to the hospital to see them in bed. Oh! That was the strangest sight! The explosion had blown the coal into their skin, you know. Their faces were exactly like lumps of coal.
Glöwr o Gwmafan, ganed tua 1900
Cwmafan miner, born around 1900

Dwi'n cofio'r danchwa ofnadwy 'na'n Gresford. Difrifol yndoedd? Odd 'ne gimint â tri wedi'u lladd mewn un teulu'n Rhos. Odd 'i'n adeg ofnadwy. Na'i byth anghofio nene. On i'n nabod lot ohonyn nw. Dros i ddau gant 'di câl 'u lladd 'ne'n do? Adeg ofnadwy.

I remember that awful explosion at Gresford. It was awful, wasn't it? As many as three were killed in one family in Rhos. It was a terrible time. I'll never forget that. I knew many of them. Over two hundred were killed there, weren't they? A terrible time.
Gwraig o Rosllannerchrugog, ganed 1911
Rhosllannerchrugog woman, born 1911

Dyddiau Blin *Hard Times*

Torfeydd yn aros am newyddion yng Nglofa'r Universal, Senghennydd, wedi'r danchwa a laddodd dros 430 o lowyr, Hydref 1913
Crowds waiting for news at Universal Colliery, Senghenydd, after the explosion in which over 430 miners were killed, October 1913

We were more or less living with death every day. Because there wasn't a week passing by, there was someone being injured, someone being killed. There was always that tragedy hanging over. I think it drew the families close together. That was my experience. I felt that as a child. That there was something hanging over us all the time.

Gwraig o Lwynypia, ganed 1904
Llwynypia woman, born 1904

'Sa rywun yn gweud 'Ma ryw anap wedi dicwdd!', a 'sa pobun mâs nawr yn y strît yn watshan beth odd wedi digwdd. A'dd ryw ffordd 'da nw o gario, chwel. 'Sa dyn yn câl i gario lan ar y stretshar ar yr ysgwdd, odd hwnna'n golygu nag odd a wedi câl cyment â 'na o anap. Ond os ôn nw'n cario lawr, odd hynny'n golygu bo' nw'n gorffod mynd yn garcus iawn, a bod e wedi câl anap yn wâth. A 'na'r peth ofnadw weti'ny, 'sa'r cap ar ben. Odd hwnna'n golygu bod y dyn wedi marw.

Somebody would say 'There's been an accident!' And everybody would be out on the street watching what happened. And they had a way of carrying, you see. If a man was carried on the stretcher up at shoulder level, that meant that he hadn't had that much of an injury. But if they were carrying low, that meant that they had to go very carefully, and that he'd been injured more seriously. But the awful thing was if the man's cap was on top. That meant that the man had died.

Gwraig o Resolfen, ganed 1902
Resolven woman, born 1902

Cysur a phrofedigaeth, Senghennydd, 1913
Comfort and distress, Senghenydd, 1913

Dyddiau Blin *Hard Times*

Angladd rhai a laddwyd yn y drychineb ym Mhwll y Darren, y Deri, 1909
Funeral of some of the victims of the disaster at Darren Colliery, Deri, 1909

O' ne ddwrnod mawr, angladd amser honno. O' ne ddigon o weinidogion i gymyd gwasaneth yn y tŷ adeg honno. Ddim yn y capel, yn y tŷ wastad. A plât ar y bwr', a 'chi'n rhoi rw ddarn tair ne chwe cheniog. 'Chydig iawn 'se'n gallu sbario swllt. Odd nene i helpu at angladd y person odd wedi mynd. Meddwl am goliars yn câl 'u lladd yn ifinc. Odd gwraig yn mynd allan i olchi amser honno i gadw'r teulu. Meddwl amdani yn gweithio'n galed yn y cartre a gorod mynd allan i olchi i rywun am ryw swllt er mwyn cal digon o fwyd yn tŷ. Ofnadwy'n doedd? O' ne fawr o *bensions* yn câl 'u rhoi o gwbwl 'ramser honno.

It was a big event, a funeral in those days. There were enough ministers to take the service in the house then. Not in the chapel, but in the house always. And a plate on the table - you'd give a thruppenny bit or sixpence. Very few could spare a shilling. That was to help towards the cost of the dead man's funeral. You think of colliers dying young. The wife had to go out washing to keep the family. You think of her having to work hard in the home and then having to go out to wash for someone else for a shilling or so, just to have enough food in the house. It was awful, wasn't it? There were very few pensions to be had in those days.

Gwraig o Rosllannerchrugog, ganed 1911
Rhosllannerchrugog woman, born 1911

In Memory
Of those who lost their lives in the
Sad Colliery Disaster at Deri on Friday, Oct 29, 1909.

1.—Wm. T. Bowen, manager, Hanbury Lodge, Bargoed.
2.—D1. Lewis, manager, Pengam.
3.—Wm. Edwards, contractor, Deri.
4.—Gomer Griffiths, overman, Gilfach Street, Bargoed.
5.—David Morgan, fireman, Fleur-de-Lis.
6.—Joseph Vincent (18), single, 6, Bute Terrace, Brithdir.
7.—John Tovey, (16), collier boy, Bailey Street, Deri.
8.—Harry Edwards (19), Mill Street, Deri.
9.—David Edwards (24), New Road, Deri.
10.—Daniel McCarthy, Cross Street, Deri.
11.—Harry Barker, Bailey Street, Deri.
12.—Morgan Coombes, Watson's Road, Deri.
13.—Ambrose Jones, Maesybryn House, Deri.
14.—Ernest Roberts, 5, Bailey Street, Deri.
15.—Lewis Morgan, Darran Cottages, Deri.
16.—John Evans (18), Bargoed Terrace, Deri.
17.—James Weeks (24), Chapel Street, Deri.
18.—William Brown, Cambrian Road, Deri.
19.—John Morgan, Bronwen Terrace, Deri.
20.—David Jenkins, New Road, Deri.
21.—Charles Vaughan, Brecon Terrace, Deri.
22.—Edward Cleavey, Chapel Street, Deri.
23.—William Davies, Bailey Street, Deri.
24.—John Baragwonit'), Bargoed Terrace, Deri.
25.—John John, Cefn Road, Deri.
26.—Evan Prosser, 3, Rees Road, Pencoed Vochriw.

Rest In Peace.

PERCY S PHILLIPS, PRINTER, BARGOED.

Dyddiau Blin *Hard Times*

Cronfa'r Arglwydd Faer ar gyfer glowyr mewn angen: adroddiad a gyhoeddwyd yn *The Sphere*, 1929
The Lord Mayor's fund for distressed miners: report published in The Sphere, *1929*

Well then in nineteen twenty nine I think it was, or thirty, this colliery closed down. So it was over now for everybody. They were dependent on this place, this area. It was all Bonville's Court pit. Once that closed well that was the end of it. There was nothing now but starvation. And that was a terrible time. Unemployment. Well we were all unemployed. And I thought 'What on earth can I do?'

Glöwr o Saundersfoot, ganed 1902
Saundersfoot miner, born 1902

39

Dyddiau Blin *Hard Times*

Glowyr Trehafod yn pigo glo yn ystod streic y Cambrian Combine, 1910-11
Trehafod miners picking coal during the Cambrian Combine strike, 1910-11

Ceson ni bedwar streic. A odd dim dima'n dod o un man, cofiwch. A beth odd yn gwŷr ni'n goffod neud odd mynd lan y *patches*, i ni gel glo at y tæn. Lan 'na ar y mynydd, a shinco, a cwnnu'r glo lan o bwcad. Odd plwyf i gael. Cel papura ôn nw o'r plwyf. 'Plwyf' ôn ni'n galw hwnna. Y *supplementary* 'yn man nw'n galw e - ma enw neis arno nawr. Ond ceson ni ddim o fa ariôd. Chi'n gwpod pam? Achos on ni wedi mynd miwn am yn tŷ bach. Os ten ni'n moyn arian i fyw, 'se raid i ni roi *deeds* y tŷ. Bysa raid i ni fyta'r tŷ. A pan 'sen ni'n byta'r tŷ, wel 'na fe. 'Se dim 'da ni. Buodd *soup kitchens* yn Hebron man 'yn. Yn y festri. Eth 'y ngwr i ganu i gal dod â arian i'r *soup kitchens*. Llawn sharabang o nw wedi mynd lawr mor belled â Milford Haven. I bob man. On nw'n canu ar sgwær Carfyrddin. Odd organ bach 'da nw. Mynd a gobitho. Odd dim llaish 'da Stephen pan dath e nôl. Wath on nw wedi canu cymint.

We had four strikes. And not a penny was coming from anywhere. The men had to go up the patches, for us to have coal for the fire. Up there on the mountain, lifting the coal up in a bucket. You could go on the parish. They used to get papers from the parish. They call it 'supplementary' now - there's a nice name for it now. But we never got it. You know why? Because we had gone in for our own little house. If we'd wanted money to live, we'd have had to surrender the deeds of the house. We'd have had to eat the house. And once you'd done that, well, that was it. We'd have nothing. There were soup kitchens here in Hebron. In the vestry. My husband went singing to make money for the soup kitchens. A charabangful of them went down as far as Milford Haven. Everywhere. They sang on Carmarthen square. They had a little organ. They'd go and hope for the best. Stephen didn't have a voice when he came back, because they'd been singing such a lot.

Gwraig o Ddowlais, ganed 1893
Dowlais miner's wife, born 1893

Dyddiau Blin *Hard Times*

Bwydo plant yn ystod streic y Cambrian Combine, 1910-11
A soup kitchen during the Cambrian Combine strike, 1910-11

Glowyr di-waith yn casglu glo, patshys Tredegar, diwedd y 1920au
Unemployed miners getting coal, Tredegar patches, late 1920s

Dyddiau Blin *Hard Times*

Plant Rhondda ym Mharc Chwaraeon Dinas, 1930au
Rhondda children at Dinas Recreation Ground, 1930s

Odd 'i'n amsar ofnadw yn y 20s, amsar wedi'r Ryfal. Tu 'wnt. Odd diweithdra, a odd rai'n mynd i ffwrdd, chimpod, gwa'nol fanna i weithio. A bu rai lan yn Llundan yn canu, chi'n gwpod. A'dd plant bach yn dod i'r ysgol, 'en *jerseys* odd gita nw, a *daps* ar 'u trâd nw. Odd a'n druenus.

Gwraig o Bont-rhyd-y-fen, ganed 1899

It was an awful time in the 20s, the period after the War. Beyond. There was unemployment, and some moved away, you know, to different places to work. And some had been up in London singing, you know. And little children were coming to school in old jerseys and daps on their feet. It was pitiful.

Pont-rhyd-y-fen woman, born 1899

Dyddiau Blin *Hard Times*

Band Jas yn Ne Cymru, 1930au. Yn ystod y Dirwasgiad, trefnid gorymdeithiau a chystadlaethau bandiau jas er mwyn codi arian a chalonnau

A South Wales Jazz Band, 1930s. In the depressed inter-war years, jazz band parades and competitions were organised to raise money and spirits

I âth cricyn onon ni - bythdi ddwsan a 'annar o ni o'ma chwel lan i Llundin - 'na'r amsar bythdi 1926. Buas i lan 'na am byti betar mlynadd ag ôn i'n myn' lawr i Charing Cross. Ag os nag och chi yn y cwrdd cwartar awr cyn bo'r cwrdd yn dechra, celich chi ddim lle i ishta lawr. *Packed* acha nos Sul. Nôl yn y 20s, *early* 30s fforna chwel. Âth 'na gannodd a milodd mâs o Gymru pyr'ny. I Llundin, Coventry a Birmingham - mâs o'r wlad 'yn chwel.

A lot of us went - about a dozen and a half from here up to London. That was the time, about 1926. I was up there for about four years, and I used to go down to Charing Cross. If you weren't in the chapel a quarter of an hour before the service started, you wouldn't find a place to sit down. It was packed on a Sunday night. Back in the 20s, early 30s. Hundreds of thousands went out of Wales at that time. To London, Coventry and Birmingham. Out of this country.

Gŵr o Bont-rhyd-y-fen, ganed tua 1900
Pont-rhyd-y-fen man, born about 1900

Brwydro 'Nôl *Fighting Back*

Glowyr yn aros i fynd i gyfarfod yn Theatr yr Empire, Tonypandy, Tachwedd 1910, yn ystod streic y Cambrian Combine
Miners waiting to go into a mass meeting at the Empire Theatre, Tonypandy, November 1910, during the Cambrian Combine strike

Why can't the people of this world reap some of the benefit of what's been provided by God? That coal was put there for something, oil was put there for something. But why are people being deprived of having the benefits? Why aren't you entitled to some of that and if you are working for it, why shouldn't you have it? You're entitled to it because there's thousands in this country today who have never done a day's work from the womb to the tomb. But I bet you that they're perhaps ten times, twenty times, a hundred times better off financially than you or me and they've never done nothing to produce it... I was quite prepared for my boss to have three suits of clothes for my one. But let me have one when I wanted it or a pair of boots.

Glöwr o Saundersfoot, ganed 1902
Saundersfoot miner, born 1902

Wi'n cofio yn grotan yn darllin pamffled Keir

Brwydro 'Nôl *Fighting Back*

Hardie - odd 'Nad yn prynu nw chimpod – A wi'n cofio atnod Keir Hardie *"The vales shall be raised and the mountains shall be brought low."* Gel fwy o gydraddoldeb ŷch chi'n gwpod.

I remember as a child reading Keir Hardie's pamphlet – Father used to buy them, you know – and I remember Keir Hardie's saying "The vales shall be raised and the mountains shall be brought low." To get more equality, you know.

Gwraig o Bont-rhyd-y-fen, ganed 1899
Pont-rhyd-y-fen woman, born 1899

45

Brwydro 'Nôl *Fighting Back*

Cyfarfod Llafur yng Nghwmafan, 1929
Labour meeting, Cwmavon, 1929

On i'n cymryd *interest* mawr yn *politics* wetini. *Trade unions* cwbwl. Off bob nos. *Meetings, politics, ILP* - wi'm 'bod beth odd a gyd pyrny. Keir Hardie'n dod rownd 'ma'n amal. On i ar 'i ôl e wetini. Duw Duw! Odd y 'ngwraig i ar weiars!... A wi'n cofio bois, wi'n cofio Arthur Horner a reina'n dod yn gynta. Ond odd 'na fechgyn wedi bod yn partói'r tir cyn 'ynny. Noah Ablett a T.I. Mardy Jones a lot o nw felna. A'dd lot o *local men* yn weddol o fyw mewn *politics*. A wth gwrs odd wnna'n partói'r lle i Arthur Horner i ddod. A dæth Arthur bach 'na, a Arthur rows y matshyn i'r lle. A 'ddar 'ny *Little Moscow* odd 'i.

I started taking a great interest in politics then. Trade unions, the lot. I was off every night - meetings, politics, ILP - I don't know what it all was then. Keir Hardie came round here often. I was following after him then. Good gosh! My wife was on pins! And I remember boys - I remember Arthur Horner and that lot coming here first. But there'd been boys here preparing the ground before that. Noah Ablett and T.I. Mardy Jones and others like that. And many local men were active in politics. And of course, that prepared the way for Arthur Horner to come. And little Arthur came, and he put a match to the place. And it's been Little Moscow since.

Glöwr o Ferndale, ganed 1882
Ferndale miner, born 1882

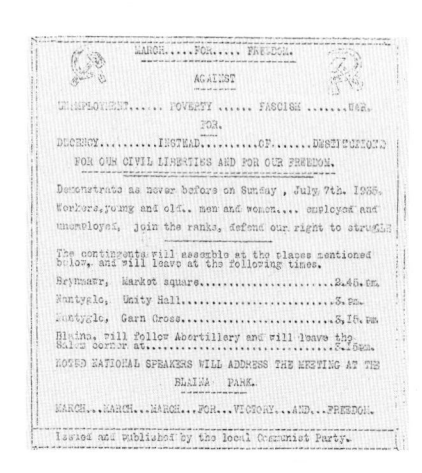

Tro ar Fyd *A Different World*

As far as I'm concerned every colliery can close. Because they hold very bad memories. Explosions - I've known explosions happening in the collieries here, as many as fourteen, fifteen men being killed in the matter of a flash. And those leaving families behind. They're sad memories, but those were the very times when people clung. Clung to each other.

Gwraig o Lwynypia, ganed 1904
Llwynypia woman, born 1904

It's entirely different now. Good old days they were. Happy days...

Gwr o Ben-y-graig, ganed 1906
Pen-y-graig man, born 1908

They had the working class where they wanted them, and that's right there, under the thumb. No question about it. That the working class were oppressed. Houses right up against the factories. Terrible life, you know. But we survived. We survived.

Gŵr o Donypandy, ganed 1906
Tonypandy man, born 1906

Datgymalu Glofa'r Naval, Pen-y-graig, 1960au
Naval Colliery, Pen-y-graig, being dismantled, 1960s

Tro ar Fyd *A Different World*

Y dram olaf cyn cau Glofa National, Wattstown, 21 Tachwedd 1968
The last tram of coal before closing National Colliery, Wattstown, 21 November 1968

Ma byw 'di dod yn well heddiw, ond 'den ni'n dlawd mewn pethe erill, yden.

Living has become easier today, but we're poorer in other things.

Gwraig o Rosllannerchrugog, ganed 1911
Rhosllannerchrugog woman, born 1911

It's funny when you think of it, innit? How things have changed, in my time, innit? Now isn't it funny how things do alter...

Gwraig o Lwynypia, ganed 1895
Llwynypia woman, born 1895

The only thing I can see constant in life is change, perpetual change...

Glöwr o Flaen-cwm, ganed tua 1890
Blaen-cwm miner, born about 1890

48